MICHAEL J. DONAHUE

I WISH I SAID THAT !

Best Wishes!

— Capt. Mike
(May 2021)

MICHAEL J. DONAHUE

I WISH I SAID THAT !

Over 1,000 of the best, funniest & wittiest quotes for every Occasion

Michael J. Donahue

captainmiked.com

captainmiked14@gmail.com

"I Wish I Said That"

 Published in the United States by Mi Sun's LLC

Library of Congress Catalog-in-Publication Data
Michael J Donahue

"I Wish I Said That"

ISBN: 978-0-9885132-1-1

The book covers were designed by Gail Brown and Alfredo Guttierez.
The photo on the back cover is by Caroline Warner

For ordering or further information, please contact us at:

captainmiked.com

captainmiked14@gmail.com

To my loving wife, Mi Sun

"When I look into her eyes
I know what kind of man
I want to be."

Table of Contents

Acknowledgements

I could not have completed this task without the persistent encouragement and assistance of my beautiful wife, Mi Sun. I also want thank Gail Brown for her enthusiasm and help in putting this book together. I want to thank Alfredo Gutierrez and Gail Brown again for helping to design the book cover. I also want thank Rosa Sophia for proofreading this book. I didn't realize how much help was needed to bring this book to fruition.Many loving hands went into making this project possible.

Sincerely,
Capt Michael J. Donahue

MICHAEL J. DONAHUE

I WISH I SAID THAT !

Introduction

Have you ever been to a party or a wedding where someone said something very witty, very funny or better yet, something truly memorable? Did it leave you thinking, "I wish I said that"? I know I have. All my life I,ve been fascinated with quotes. Interesting, funny, intelligent and sometimes irreverent quotes.

I remember as a fourteen-year old high school freshman, sitting in a large auditorium at the Boston Latin School, (the oldest public school the nation, est.1636). I sat waiting along with hundreds of other bored, students to watch a 1953 black & white movie,"Julius Caesar". Gazing up at the Auditorium ceiling inscribed on the frieze were names of famous alumni. I was mesmerized by the names of these famous Boston Latin School alumns, Benjamin Franklin, Ralph Waldo Emerson, John Hancock and George Santayana.The last name on the ceiling, Santayana caught my attention. It caught my attention because it was unlike any of the other Yankee-Brahmin names. I went to the Encyclopedia Britannica, and looked up the name Santayana, (This was before the age of Google). I found that George Santayana, was a poet and philosopher, born in Spain, lived in Boston, graduated from Harvard University and was quite famous in his day. He was known for among other things, a famous quote that resonated with me immediately. The quote was "Those who fail to learn the lessons of history are condemned to repeat them." I sensed this quote was special, even if as a young teenager. I did not know why? A few years later as a curious college student at the height of the Vietnam War, Santayana's words seemed almost prescient. I have thought of this quote many times throughout my life. In fact, soon after this, another local writer, Henry David Thoreau's famous quote caught my eye, while I was working at a soul-crushing job at Boston City Hall. The quote read "The mass of men lead lives of quiet desperation." That quotation haunted me throughout my young working life. It made me question, Why are we here ? What is important in life ? How do we avoid living a "Life of quiet desperation"? I decided right then and there not to end up leading a life of "quiet desperation".

Growing up in a single parent home, I think these quotes were a way of helping me to self-parent and find my own way. This also started me on an over fifty-year quest of collecting interesting, serious and often humorous quotes to ponder, use and bring up at the right occasion. I jotted these sayings down on envelopes, scraps of paper and matchbook covers. Forty years later my wife, Mi Sun found a shoe-box full of my collection of quotes. When she asked why was I saving them ? I told her that someday I hoped to put them together into book form. My wife thought it was a very good idea and could be helpful to others. She constantly prodded me to write this book and share these nuggets of information with interested readers. During the recent Pandemic I finally got around to completing this book.

I hope you find it useful, enjoyable, or perhaps inspiring you to pursue your own goals. In researching these quotes I have tried to track down the original author(s), although sometimes there seems to be more than one person to whom the individual quotes are attributed. I have tried in every case to be as accurate as possible, even though, many quotes have gone through numerous iterations and alterations. If you find any corrections, or more accurate information, please do not hesitate to enlighten me. Most of all, Enjoy !

CHAPTER ONE

Love and Marriage

"Love is like a fire,
but whether it is going to warm your heart
or burn your house down,
you never can tell."

Joan Crawford, actress

"We are most alive when we are in love."

John Updike, writer

"Love is like the wind. You can't see it,
but you can feel it. "

Nicholas Sparks, writer

"By all means marry;
if you find a good one,
you'll become happy.
If you get a bad one,
you'll become a philosopher."

Socrates, philosopher

"Instead of getting married again,
next time I'm going to find a woman I don't like
and give her a house.

Rod Stewart, singer

"Marriage is a damnably serious business,
especially in Boston."

John P. Marquand, writer, social commentary

"Regard your own selfishness
as the core problem in your marriage."

Tim Kelleher

"Never go on trips with anyone you don't love."

Ernest Hemingway, author

"Run to the rescue with love, and peace will follow."

Joaquin Phoenix (quoting his late brother, River while accepting the Academy Award for Best Actor)

"I may not be your first date, your first kiss,
or your first love:
I just want to be your last everything."

"Even the rich are hungry for love,
for being cared for,
for being wanted,
for having someone all to their own."

Mother Teresa

"If you want to change the world,
go home and love your family."

Mother Teresa

"It is better to have loved and lost
than to have never loved at all."

Alfred Lord Tennyson, poet

"I want to do to you
what springtime does to the cherry tree."

Pablo Neruda, poet

"When you look into her eyes
you know what kind of man you want to be."

"Lovers don't finally meet somewhere,
they're in each other all along."

Rumi, poet

"The heart has reasons that the mind has not."

Pascal Blaise

"The moment we begin to seek love,
love begins to seek, and save us."

Paulo Coelho

"Truth is the only ground to stand on."

"Go find yourself first, so you can also find me."

Rumi, poet

"Love is the irresistible desire to be desired."

Robert Frost, poet

"When the power of love
overcomes the love of power,
the world will know peace."

Jimi Hendrix, songwriter, musician

"Many a man has fallen in love with a girl in a light so dim he would not have chosen a suit by it."

Maurice Chevalier, actor

"The heart wants what it wants or it does not care."

Emily Dickinson

"Let there be spaces in your togetherness."

Khalil Gibran

"If you're rich, I'm single."

(Bumper sticker seen on an automobile in Palm Beach)

"If two people love each other there can be no happy end to it."

Ernest Hemingway, author

"The best thing a father can do for his children
is to love their mother."

John Wooden, legendary basketball coach

"If you want to know about a loving relationship,
go plant a garden and attend it with care.
The garden will teach you all you have to know."

Mi Sun, author, philosopher

"You told me you loved me.
So I believed you."

Mi Sun, author, philosopher

"To Love someone deeply gives you strength, being
loved by someone deeply gives you courage."

Lao Tz

"There is a candle in the heart
waiting to be lit."

Rumi, poet

"I am who I am, because you are who you are."

Rumi

"Second marriages
are the triumph of hope over experience."

George Bernard Shaw, author, playwright

"Love does not consist of gazing at each other,
but looking outward together in the same direction."

Antoine de Saint-Exupery, author

"The course of true love never did run smooth."

William Shakespeare, writer, poet

"It is awfully simple to fall in love.
It is simply awful to fall out of love."

Bess Myerson, former Miss America

"It is better to kiss your wife goodbye
and leave the house,
than leave your wife
and kiss your house goodbye."

"Unable are the loved to die,
for love is immortality."

Emily Dickinson, poet

"An archeologist is the best husband a woman can have; the older she gets the more interested he is in her."

Agatha Christie, mystery writer,
(She was married to an archeologist)

"You give me premature ventricular contractions."

(translation: "you make my heart skip a beat.")

"It sometimes helps to be a little deaf."
(Her mother's advice on marriage)

Ruth Bader Ginsburg, Supreme Court Justice

"To say goodbye is to die a little."

Raymond Chandler, Mystery writer

"Whatever our souls are made of,
yours and mine are the same."

Emily Bronte

CHAPTER TWO

ADVICE

"Never go to a Doctor
whose office plants have died."

Tom Harkins, U.S. Senator

"Those who fail to learn the lessons of history
are condemned to repeat them."

George Santayana, poet, philosopher

"Stay away from negative people.
They have a problem for every solution."

Albert Einstein

"If I had an hour to save the world, I'd spend 55 minutes to design a plan and 5 minutes to act on it."

Albert Einstein

"Be so good, they can't ignore you."

Oprah Winfrey

"If you don't like something change it.
If you can't change it,
change your attitude."

Maya Angelou, poet

"The most important single ingredient
in the formula of success
is knowing how to get along with people."

Theodore Roosevelt, U.S. President

"People first, then money, then things."

Suze Orman, financial planner

"If you can't argue the facts, argue the law,
if the law and the facts are against you,
pound the table and yell like hell."

Carl Sandburg, poet

"If you always do what you've always done,
you'll always get
what You've always got."

Ed Foreman

"Surrender what is, let go of what was,
have faith in what will be."

Sonia Ricotti, writer

"Never be defined by your past.
It was just a lesson,
not a life sentence."

Honda Kotb, TV personality

"No one can make you feel inferior without your consent."

Eleanor Roosevelt,
First Lady, Human rights activist

"A moment of patience in a moment of anger saves you a hundred moments of regret."

Bhavya Gaur, Spiritual counselor

"The best way out is always through."

Robert Frost, Poet Laureate

"Be loud about the things that are important to you"

Karen Wolrond

"Never complain, never explain."

Benjamin Disraeli, British Prime Minister

"Be careful who you trust
and tell your problems to.
Not everyone who smiles at you is your friend."

"Don't ruin a good day today
by thinking about a bad day yesterday."

"Create history, don't wait for it to happen."

Shep Gordon, film producer, talent agent

"I have a theory. I think your worst weakness can become your greatest single strength."

Barbara Corcoran, real estate entrepreneur

"Life is like a can of sardines.
Everyone is looking for the key."

"If all you can do is crawl, start crawling."

Rumi, poet

"Do something today
that your future self will thank you for."

Sean Patrick Flannery, actor

"Take time everyday to laugh, to think, to cry."

Jim Valvano, N.C. State basketball coach

"Forget the career, do the work."

Al Pacino, actor

"You're always one decision away from
a totally different life."

"Tread softly, because you tread on my dreams."

William Butler Yeats, poet

All disease begins in the gut."

Hippocrates, philosopher

"Keep your eyes on the stars,
but you're feet on the ground."

Franklin Delano Roosevelt, U.S. President

"Being it, is better than doing it or having it."

Thomas Merton, Trappist monk, author

"Weak people, revenge, strong people, forgive,
intelligent people, ignore."

Albert Einstein, physicist

"If you live everyday as if it were your last,
someday you most certainly will be right."

Steven Jobs, Apple Computer

"Don't squat with your spurs on."

Will Rogers, humorist

"It is no measure of health to be well-adjusted to a profoundly sick society."

Krishnamurti, Spiritual advisor

"We are what our thoughts have made us;
so take care about what you think.
Words are secondary.
Thoughts live;
they travel far."

Swami Vivekananda

"Advice is what we ask for
when we already know the answer,
but wish we didn't."

Erica Jong, author

"A word of advice. Don't give it."

A. J. Volicos

"Follow your intuition,
listen to your heart
and act on it.
But, when in doubt,
do nothing."

Jane Alexander, Academy Award winning actress

"Promise me you,ll always remember: you're braver than you believe, and stronger than you seem and smarter than you think."

A.A. Milne (Christopher Robin to Pooh)

"The fool doth think he is wise, but the wise man knows himself to be a fool."

William Shakespeare

"Intense personal desire is the wellspring of action."

Neville Goddard, author

"Be the person you want to meet."

"To be happy, find out what you like.
Find out what you're good at,
and learn to do it to the best of your ability."

Michael Donahue, Boat Captain

"He who lives in harmony with himself,
lives in harmony with the universe."

Marcus Aurelius, Roman emperor, philosopher

"What lies behind us and what lies before us
are tiny matters compared to what lies within us."

Ralph Waldo Emerson, philosopher, essayist

"To plant a garden is to believe in tomorrow."

Audrey Hepburn

"Mystery is not about traveling to new places,
but its about seeing.
Seeing with new eyes."

Marcel Proust, writer

"To know what you know and do not know."

Confucius

"I am the soul of the dictionary that defines me."

"Don't get mad. Getting mad only hurts.
Use that energy to to accomplish your goals."

Shep Gordon, film producer, talent agent

"When you understand that your self-worth is not determined by your net worth, then you,ll have financial freedom."

Suze Orman, financial planner

"There will be no success or real reward without risk."

Robert Mayer, author

"Look for the job you'd take, if you didn't need a job."

Warren Buffet, investor

"God knows what he is doing, even if you don't, God has a plan even if you don't."

Rhonda Rousey, Mixed Martial Arts Champion

"When in doubt, stand still."

Julie Andrews, actress

"There will be a beginning, a middle and an end."

Julie Andrews, actress
(quoting her mother regarding the pandemic)

"Nobody knows nothing."

William Goldman, screenwriter (describing Hollywood)

"Enjoy the ride - choose the right partner and decide what you really want to do in life and then do it."

Eli Wallach, actor

"You have to keep busy after all. No dog ever pissed on a moving car."

Tom Waits, singer, actor

"It's not what you look at that matters, it's what you see."

Henry David Thoreau, philosopher

"Judging a person does not define who they are. It defines who you are.

Paulo Coelho, author

"Read 500 pages a day.
That's how knowledge works.
It builds up like compound interest."

Warren Buffet, investor

"It's never too late to have a happy childhood."

Wayne Dyer, author, motivational speaker

"Take the high road, it's much less crowded."

Warren Buffet, investor

"We don,t have to be smarter than the rest.
We have to be
more disciplined than the rest."

Warren Buffet, investor

"Never invest in a business you can,t understand."

Warren Buffet, investor

"We all have two lives.
The second one starts when we realize
we only have one."

Confucius

"Be fearful when there is greed
and be greedy when there is fear."

Warren Buffet, investor

"The key to success is emotional stability."

Warren Buffet, investor

"It's a good idea to review past mistakes
before committing new ones."

Warren Buffet, investor

"The first rule is not to lose.
The second rule is not to forget the first rule."

Warren Buffet,

"Always associate yourself with people
who are better than you."

Warren Buffet, investor

"Sometimes you win, sometimes you learn."

John C. Maxwell

"Don't be sad because it's over.
Be happy that it happened."

Dr. Theodor Seuss Geisel,
(Dr. Seuss), children's author

"Failure is the condiment that gives
success it's flavor."

Truman Capote, novelist

"When the tide goes out you find out who's been
swimming naked."

Warren Buffet, investor

"Asking for advice from a financial planner
is like asking a barber
if you need a haircut."

Warren Buffet, investor

"We become what we think about most of the time,
and that's the strangest secret."

Earl Nightingale

"Only put off until tomorrow
what you are willing to die having left undone."

Pablo Picasso, artist

"Whenever you find yourself
on the side of the majority,
it is time to pause and reflect."

Mark Twain author

"If you don't find a way
to make money while you sleep,
you'll work until the day you die."

Warren Buffet, investor

"The happiest people
do not necessarily have the best things.
They simply appreciate the things they have."

Warren Buffet, investor

"Eventually all things fall into place. Until then,
laugh at the confusion, live for the moments and
know everything happens for a reason."

*Dr. Albert Schweitzer, Nobel Peace Prize winner,
humanitarian*

"The happiness in your life depends on the quality of
your thoughts."

Marcus Aurelius, Roman emperor, philosopher

"The more joy we have,
the more nearly perfect we are."

Spinoza, philosopher

"Never wrestle with a pig,
because you'll both get dirty and the pig loves it."

George Bernard Shaw, playwright

"Watch what they do, not what they say."

*Rachel Maddow, television commentator,
Rhodes Scholar*

"My mother said, you won't amount to anything
because you always procrastinate.
I said, just you wait."

Judy Tenuta, comedian

"Don't bore us, get to the chorus."

Michael Bolton, singer

"Success is being able to say no without worrying about the consequences."

Paul Newman actor, philanthropist

"There is only one success - to be able to spend your life in your own way."

"Be quick, but don't be in a hurry."

John Wooden, UCLA basketball coach

"If you can't be on time, be early."

John Wooden, UCLA basketball coach

"Make each day your masterpiece."

John Wooden, UCLA basketball coach

"Beginning is the most important part of work."

Plato, philosopher

"Don't mistake activity with achievement."

John Wooden, UCLA, basketball coach

"Don't let making a living prevent you
from making a life."

John Wooden, UCLA basketball coach

"If you don't have time to do it right,
when will you have to time do it over."

John Wooden, UCLA basketball coach

"What we know matters,
but who we are matters more."

Brene Brown, motivational speaker

"Even mistakes can be wonderful."

Robin William, comedian

"Our job is improving the quality of life,
not just delaying death."

Robin Williams, comedian

"If you see something beautiful in someone,
speak it.
One moment can change a day,
One day can change a life,
one life can change
the world."

Confucius, philosopher

"Be the reason someone believes
in the goodness of people."

Karen Salmonsohn, self-help writer

"Resentment is the poison you swallow, hoping the
other person will die."

Carrie Fisher, actress, writer

"You're only given a little spark of madness. You mustn't lose it."

Robin Williams, comedian

"You're still young, being a true loser takes years of ineptitude."

Robin Williams

"Don't ever take a fence down until you know why it was put up."

Robert Frost, Poet Laureate

"You don't get a second chance. Life ain't no Nintendo game."

Eminem

"You've got enemies? Good. That means you actually stood for something in your life."

Eminem

"Love is evil spell it backwards. I'll show ya."

Eminem

"My wife likes to comfort the afflicted
and afflict the comfortable."

Michael Donahue, Boat Captain

"Nothing you do for your children is wasted."

Garrison Keillor, writer, raconteur

"Never cut what you can untie."

Robert Frost, poet Laureate

"It is better to have permanent income
than to be fascinating."

Oscar Wilde, writer, playwright

"The truth is rarely pure and never simple."

Oscar Wilde

"I believe in looking reality straight in the eye and denying it."

Oscar Wilde

"The noblest art is making someone happy."

P. T. Barnum, founder, Barnum & Bailey Circus

"I am not young enough to know everything."

Oscar Wilde

"Things turn out best for the people who make the best of the way things turn out."

Robert Frost, Poet Laureate

"I never think of the future, it comes soon enough."

Albert Einstein, physicist, Nobel Prize in Physics

"When you repeat a mistake, it is not a mistake anymore: it is a decision."

Paulo Coelho, writer

"Laugh when you can, apologize when you should and let go of what you cannot change."

"If you only walk on sunny days you,ll never get to your destination."

Paulo Coelho, writer

"If you want to see a rainbow, you have to see the rain."

Paulo Coelho,writer

"The world is changed by your example,
not your opinion."

Paulo Coelho,writer

"Haters are confused admirers who can't understand
why everyone else likes you."

Paulo Coelho, writer

"If you want to live a happy life, tie it to a goal, not
to people or objects."

Albert Einstein, Nobel Prize in Physics

"The best way to cheer yourself up
is to try to cheer somebody else up."

Mark Twain, writer, raconteur

"The most important thing is to enjoy your life -
to be happy It's all that matters."

Audrey Hepburn, actress, humanitarian

"Very little is needed to make a happy life. It is all within yourself, within your thinking."

Marcus Aurelius, Roman emperor, philosopher

"Rules for happiness; something to do, someone to love, something to hope for."

Immanuel Kant, philosopher

"You're at your best
when you don't know what you're doing."

Paul Stanley, KISS, (on being in the Zone)

"It's not the answer that enlightens,
but the question."

Eugene Ionesco, playwright, dramatist

"Do not wait until the conditions are perfect to begin. Beginning makes the conditions perfect."

Alan Cohen, businessman

"No one ever dies
wishing they'd spent more time at the office."

Malcolm Forbes, entrepreneur, publisher

"Pressure is something you feel
when you don't know what you're doing."

Chuck Knoll, Pittsburgh Steelers,
(4 time Super Bowl winning coach)

"Good things come to those who hustle."

Chuck Noll, Pittsburgh Steelers coach

"We don,t stop playing because we grow old; we grow old because we stop playing."

George Bernard Shaw

"A consultant; that's what you call a person
who is unemployed."

"My son is an "Entrepreneur", that's what you're called when you don't have a job."

Ted Turner, Founder of CNN
(First 24 hour news service)

"See the face of God in everyone."

St. Catherine Laboure

"When you don't know what you're doing, fake it."

Jill Shalvis, Author

"Fake it, til you make it."

Slogan used in Alcoholics Anonymous
and other 12-Step Groups

"One day at a time."

Slogan used in Alcoholics Anonymous
and other 12-Step Groups

"Easy does it."

Slogan used in Alcoholics Anonymous and other 12-Step Groups

"First things first."

Slogan used in Alcoholics Anonymous and other 12-St Groups

"You cannot shake hands with a clenched fist."

Indira Ghandi, Prime Minister, India

"Do not mind anything that anyone tells you about anyone else.
Judge everyone and everything for yourself."

Henry James, author

"Learning never exhausts the mind."

Leonardo da Vinci, polymath

"Honesty is the first chapter in the book of wisdom."

Thomas Jefferson, US President

"All paid jobs absorb and degrades the mind."

Aristotle, philosopher

"The only place where success comes before work is in the dictionary."

Vince Lombardi, Green Bay Packers coach

"Sometimes the light at the end of the tunnel is an oncoming train."

"It is always darker just before it goes completely black."

John McCain, U.S. Senator

"Listen to everyone, then do what you want."

Diane von Furstenberg, fashion designer

"If you can't do what you do, do what you can."

Jon Bon Jovi, musician (while volunteering washing dishes during the pandemic)

"Choice not chance determines destiny."

"If you ain't, the lead dog, the view never changes."

"We may have all come over on different boats,
but we're in the same boat now."

Martin Luther King Jr., civil rights leader

"Do or do not. There is no try."

Yoda, (from "Star-wars")

"Don't let perfect be the enemy of perfectly good."

"I have a simple philosophy, fill what's empty, empty what's full. Scratch what itches."

Alice Roosevelt Longworth,
eldest daughter of President Theodore Roosevelt.

"I'll try anything once."

Alice Roosevelt Longworth,
(on becoming pregnant at age 41)

"Always do more than is required of you."

General George S.Patton

"Choose a job you love
and you'll never have to work a day in your life."

Confucius

"There are 86,400 seconds in a day.
It's up to you to decide what to do with the day."

Dr. Elvin Seema

"It's hard not to like someone
once you know their story."

Mr. Rogers, Public Television Host

"Would the boy in you be proud of the man you,ve become."

Lawrence J. Peter, professor,
founder of the Peter Principle

"Always find time for the things that make you feel happy to be alive."

Nanno

"Don't look back,
something may be catching up to you."

Satchel Paige, baseball legend

"In dealing with others,
always underpromise and overdeliver."

Michael J. Donahue, Boat Captain

First friend: "It's nice to see you."
Second friend: "I'd rather be seen than be viewed."

"Absorb what is useful, reject what is useless,
add what is essential of your own."

Bruce Lee, Martial Arts Expert

"Remember, failure is your friend.
It is a major tool of progress."

Nina Foch, actress

"Have a lifelong interest in reading since reading
is the key to knowledge."

Walter Cronkite, legendary television news anchor

"Be a giver, not a taker."

Ezra Stone, director

"Believe half of what you see,
and none of what you hear."

Joe Don Baker, actor

"Forgive others not because they deserve forgiveness,
but because you deserve peace."

"Not all who wander are lost."

J. R. Tolkien , author

"Think about this, big things start small."

Jeff Bezos, founder, Amazon

"Every day commit something to memory:
a poem, a saying, some new words,
a foreign language.
You will be rich in wisdom and wit."

Alice Ilchman, President, Sarah Lawrence College

"The most important thing is to learn how to learn."

John Naismith, author, Megatrends

"Life is a funny thing, the harder you work the luckier you get."

*Melvin Simon, Simon Group,
shopping mall developer*

"Work like you don't need the money.
Love like you've never been hurt.
Dance like nobody's watching."

Satchel Paige, Baseball Legend

"The secret to success is to always
take pride in what you do
and do more than you are expected to do.

Sidney Sheldon, novelist

"Care about people not things. Remember that
things can be replaced, people can,t."

Judith Crist, film critic

"Life expands or shrinks in proportion
to one's courage."

Anais Nin

"The best way to get your point across
is to entertain."

George B. Shaw, playwright

"The higher a monkey climbs
the more you see of its behind."

General Joseph Stillwell

"Experience is simply the name we give our mistakes."

Oscar Wilde, playwright

"Hypocrisy is the compliment we give to virtue."

Oscar Wilde, playwright

"The mass of men lead lives of quiet desperation."

Henry David Thoreau, writer

CHAPTER THREE

Kindness

"Before you speak, let your words
pass through these three gates:
Is it true? Is it necessary? Is it kind?

Rumi, poet

"The smallest act of kindness is worth more than the greatest intention."

Khalil Gibran, writer, philosopher

"Be kind to everyone on the way up; you'll meet the same people on the way down."

Wilson Mizner, playwright

"You cannot do a kindness too soon,
for you never know how soon
it will be too late."

Ralph Waldo Emerson, writer,

"Together we can change the world,
just one random act of kindness at a time."

Ron Hall, author

"If you can't be kind, at least be vague."

Dave Powers, personal aide to President Kennedy

Be kind whenever it's possible. It's always possible."

Dalai Lama

"Kindness is the beginning and end of the law."

Hebrew proverb

"No act of kindness, no matter how small,
is ever wasted."

Aesop, Greek fabulist

"Every now and then,
without anyone knowing about it,
do something kind for someone who needs
and doesn't expect it."

Brett Butler, comedienne

"My religion is very simple.
My religion is kindness."

Dalai Lama

"A warm smile
is the universal language of kindness."

William Arthur Ward, writer

"Kindness is the language the deaf can hear and the blind can see."

Mark Twain, author, raconteur

"Always be a little kinder than necessary."

Jamie Barrie, author of "Peter Pan"

CHAPTER FOUR

Wisdom

"People will forget what you did.
People will forget what you said,
but people will never forget
how you made them feel"

Maya Angelou

"Who knows, does not tell."

"If you want people to listen to you, listen to them."

"A man who has wasted an hour of time has not discovered the value of life."

Charles Darwin, anthropologist

"Education is not preparation for life,
education is life itself."

John Dewey, educator

"He who can does, he who cannot teaches."

George Bernard Shaw

"From grief, learn strength."

Mao Tse-Tung

"I judge myself not by what I have,
but what I give to others."

Corinthians 4:31

"Ask yourself, do you think it will matter twenty
years from now."

Jack Turner, founder of Soundings Magazine

"Personality is what you do when everybody's looking. Character is what you do when nobody's looking."

"Yesterday I was clever and wanted to change the world. Today I am wise and want to change myself."

Rumi, poet

"One thing that I know, that I know nothing. This is the source of my wisdom."

Socrates

"Wisdom begins in wonder."

Socrates

"Live in the present, remember the past, fear not the future."

"Remember, today is the tomorrow
you worried about yesterday."

Dale Carnegie

"All things truly wicked start from innocence."

Ernest Hemingway

"Absence of evidence is not evidence of absence."

"Virtue is its own revenge."

E. Y. (Yip) Harburg, composer

"Nothing changes, if nothing changes"

"When someone shows you who they are,
believe them the first time."

Maya Angelou, writer

"The oldest, shortest - "yes" and "no" are those which require the most thought."

Pythagoras, mathematician

"Knowledge is knowing a tomato is a fruit; Wisdom is not putting it in a fruit salad."

"Even a broken clock is right twice a day."

Arnie von Ebner-Eshebach

"I hear and I forget. I see and I remember. I do and I understand."

Confucius

"Happiness is a choice, not a result."

Ralph Marston, motivational speaker

"Character is how you treat those who can do nothing for you."

"We're all in the gutter, it's just that some of us are looking up at the stars."

Oscar Wilde, playwright

"Live simply so that others may simply live."

Elizabeth Seton, first American to be canonized as a Saint

"It is good to think, better to look, best to look without thinking."

Goethe, philosopher

"You don't learn what's important till it breaks down."

Heidegger, philosopher

"Life is not a dress rehearsal."

Rose Tremain

"Be careful of others. Sugar and salt look the same."

"Hurt people, hurt people."

"I will live my life, not perform it."

"Never let yesterday take up too much of today."

Tex Schram, General Manager,
Dallas Cowboys football team

"Forget the failures. Keep the lessons."

Dalai Lama

"Don't let the behavior of others
destroy your inner peace."

Dalai Lama

"The past is your lesson, the present is your gift, the future is your motivation."

"Not everything that counts can be counted."

Dennis Burkett

"Imitation is the sincerest form of flattery."

Charles Caleb Cotton

"When you know better, you do better."

Maya Angelou, author

"When everybody is somebody,
then nobody is anybody.

Gilbert & Sullivan

"A good deed never goes unpunished."

Gore Vidal, author

"Excellence is not the result of a singular act, but a constant habit."

Aristotle

"Experience teaches you to recognize a mistake when you've made it again."

"Courage is not the absence of fear,
it is the ability to act in the presence of fear."

Bruce Lee, Martial Arts Expert

"Fill what's empty, empty what's full
and scratch where it itches.

Talullah Bankhead, actress

"For want of a nail, the shoe was lost.
For want of the shoe, the horse was lost.
For want of the horse, the rider was lost.
For want of the rider the battle was lost.
For want of the battle the kingdom was lost,
and all for the want of a nail."

Ben Franklin

"Success is like smoking, it probably won't harm you
if you don't inhale."

"Experience is the name
everyone gives to their mistakes."

Oscar Wilde

"Experience is learning from your mistakes,
wisdom is learning from someone else's mistakes."

"A mind is like an open wound, if it's too open,
it's likely to get an infection."

"The only reason the engineer is good
is because of curiosity."

John Thompson

"All truly great thoughts are conceived by walking."

Frederick Nietzsche

"Do something, lead, follow or get out of the way."

Ted Turner, founder, CNN

"It's a trade secret, but I'll tell you anyway,
all healing is self healing."

Dr. Albert Schweitzer, physician, Nobel Prize Winner

CHAPTER FIVE

Stupidity

"The problem with the world is
that intelligent people are full of doubt,
while the the stupid ones are full of confidence."

Charles Bukowski, author, poet

"We're all born ignorant, but one must work very hard to remain stupid."

Ben Franklin

"When a stupid man is doing something he is ashamed of, he always declares it is his duty."

George Bernard Shaw

"It's a travesty of a mockery of a sham."

Woody Allen, Director, actor

"Any fool can make a rule."

Henry David Thoreau

"It's dangerous to be sincere unless you're also stupid."

George Bernard Shaw, playwright

"Being ignorant is not so much as being unwilling to learn."

Ben Franklin

"There is no expedient to which a man will resort to avoid thinking."

Sir Joshua Reynolds

"Half the world is composed of people who have something to say and can't, the other half who have nothing to say and keep saying it."

Robert Frost

"Our nation is turning into an idiocracy."

Neil deGrasse Tyson, physicist

"You can't fix stupid."

Ron White, comedian

"The doctor can bury his mistakes,
but the architect can only cover them with vines."

Frank Lloyd Wright, Architect

"The world will not be destroyed by mean people,
but by stupid people."

Sir Bertrand Russell, Nobel Prize in Literature

"Useful Idiots"

Josef Stalin, Russian Dictator

"He's learning to say hello, when he should be learning how to say goodbye "

(about Barry Bonds,the MVP baseball player)

"The basis of optimism is sheer terror."

Oscar Wilde, playwright

"If his IQ slips any lower we,ll have to water him twice a day."

Molly Ivins, Political columnist

"Why do it right, when you can do it yourself."

Robert Thurman's son's comment on his father building his own house.

CHAPTER SIX

Humor

"I want to be cremated.
It's my last chance to have a smoking hot body."

"He's so narrow-minded
he can see through a keyhole with both eyes."

Molly Ivins, columnist

"A quail is a chicken with a press agent."

"The British are obsessed with cooking, but are incapable of cooking.

"Washington is like Hollywood for ugly people."

"He couldn't ad-lib a fart at a bean supper."

Johnny Carson,talk show host
(describing Chevy Chase's inability to ad-lib)

"Never have children, only grandchildren."

Gore Vidal, author

"Half of what we're teaching in medical school is wrong. The problem is we don't know which half."

Dr. Lydia Kang, author of "Quackery"

"It's like trying to teach Hindu to a beagle."

Michael J. Donahue, Boat Captain

"Dancing is a vertical expression
of a horizontal desire."

Cole Porter, composer

"We started off trying to set up
a small anarchist community,
but nobody would obey the rules."

"Death is life's way of telling you to slow down."

"Cocaine is God's way of telling you
you're making too much money."

Richard Pryor, comedian

"My mother never saw the irony in calling me
a son of a bitch."

Jack Nicholson, actor

"The noblest of all dogs is the hot-dog;
it feeds the hand that bites it."

"When people ask me how many people work here,
I say about a third of them."

Lisa Kennedy

"Those who believe in telekinesis, raise my hand."

Kurt Vonnegut, writer

"I went to a restaurant that said,
'Breakfast Anytime',
so I ordered French Toast during the renaissance."

Steven Wright, comedian

"A clear conscience is usually
a sign of a bad memory."

Steven Wright, comedian

"The only difference between a tax man
and a taxidermist
is that taxidermist leaves the skin."

Mark Twain, author, raconteur

"Inside every fat book is a thin book
trying to get out."

"My psychiatrist told me I was crazy, so I told him I
wanted a second opinion. He said okay,
you're ugly too."

Rodney Dangerfield, comedian

"I went to a fight the other night
and a hockey game broke out."

Rodney Dangerfield, comedian

"Money's tight, times are hard,
Here's your f*cking birthday card."

"If you're not at the dinner
you're probably on the menu."

"A world class, spectacular, colossal pain in the ass."

Robert De Niro,
(describing his good friend Dustin Hoffman at the Kennedy Center Honors ceremony)

"It is better to look good than to feel good."

Billy Crystal, (on SNL imitating Fernando Lamas)

"How could you believe me when I told you
that I loved you, when you know
I've been a liar all my life."

Burton Lane, composer

"Every word she writes is a lie,
including *if* and *but*."

Mary McCarthy, writer
(describing Lillian Hellman to Dick Cavett)

"If they call it Tourist Season,
why can't we shoot them."

(Bumper sticker on an auto in Woods Hole, Ma.)

"I'm as pure as the driven slush."

Talullah Bankhead, actress

"Dumber than a taste-tester a lead paint factory."

"Ever since young men have owned motorcycles,
incest has been dying out."

Max Frisch,

"Ladies and gentlemen, start your coffins."

Jim Murray, L.A. Times sports columnist,
re: Indianapolis 500

"Never eat more than you can lift."

Miss Piggy

"You never know how many friends you have until you rent a summer cottage."

Friends, tv comedy

"I Don't want to set the world on fire,
I just want to keep my nuts warm."

from a sign on a roasted chestnut vendor's stand in
Times Square NYC

"Eagles may soar,
but weasels don't get sucked into jet engines."

Steven Wright, comedian

"If at first you don't succeed, then skydiving is definitely not for you."

Steven Wright, comedian

"I think it's wrong
that only one company makes Monopoly."

Steven Wright, comedian

"A friend will help you move.
A good friend will help you move a body."

"When you have a body in your trunk it's a good idea not to break the speed limit."

"The number one fear in life is public speaking,
the number two fear is death."

Jerry Seinfeld, comedian

"People say doing nothing is impossible,
but I do nothing everyday."

A.A. Milne

"I want to die like my grandfather died.
Peacefully, in his sleep.
Not like the other three people
screaming in the car."

Joey Adams, comedian

"It's such a fine line between stupid and clever."

from the movie "This is Spinal Tap", directed by Rob Reiner, United States, produced by Karen Murphy, 1984

"Buffet: a French word that means,
get up and get it yourself."

"If you go to bed in your fireplace.
You'll sleep like a log.

Ellen DeGeneres, comedienne

"Never follow someone else's path,
unless you're in the woods and you're lost."

Ellen DeGeneres, comedienne

"Men don't get cellulite. God might just be a man."

Rita Rudner, comedienne

"Men who drink herbal teas
are seldom serial killers."

Rita Rudner, comedienne

"I don't trust him. We're friends."

Bertolucci Brecht, playwright

"Outside every thin girl is a fat man trying to get in."

"I never gossip,
but I can give you the names
of certain people who do."

Judy Hampton

"The only time a woman really succeeds in changing a man is when he's a baby."

"Macho doesn't prove mucho."

Zsa Zsa Gabor, actress

"Change is not a four letter word, but often your reaction to it is."

Jeff Gitomer

"Drop your pants here and you'll get prompt attention."

From a sign outside a dry cleaning establishment.

"I'm an atheist and I have God to thank for it.

"If only I had a little humility, I'd be perfect.

Ted Turner, founder, CNN

"What a terrible round of golf.
I only hit two good balls all day,
and that was when I stepped
on a rake in the bunker."

Lee Trevino, golf professional

"He's so uptight, when he farts
only dogs can hear it."

"You have my complete,
undivided, partial attention."

"I figure you have the same chance
of winning the lottery
whether you play or not."

Fran Leibowitz, writer

"Our bait is guaranteed to catch fish or die trying."

(*From a sign outside a Florida bait shop)*

"I don't believe in astrology - of course,
that's very typical of Leo's."

Wendy Morgan, writer

"When you spend an hour with a beautiful woman
it seems like a few minutes.
When you spend a few minutes with an ugly woman
it seems like an hour."

Albert Einstein
(trying to explain simply his Theory of Relativity)

"I'm a Godmother, that's a great thing to be.
She calls me God for short. I taught her that."

Ellen DeGenreres

"Beauty is skin deep,
but ugly runs clean to the bone."

Dorothy Parker, writer, satirist

"I became a policeman because I wanted to be in a
business where the customer is always wrong."

"I have an intense desire to go back to the womb, anybody's womb."

Woody Allen, comedian, director

"I don't like the fact that doctors are referred to as practicing."

"If you can't say something nice about somebody, come sit here next to me."

Alice Roosevelt Longworth, socialite

"It's like trying to herd a bunch of cats."

Overheard at a sales manager,s meeting.

"Man plans, God laughs."

"Float like a butterfly, sting like a bee."

Muhammed Ali, Heavyweight Boxing Champion

"Float like a Lepidoptera,
sting like a Hymenoptera."

*Dr. Niles Crain, "Fraser" TV comedy show,
directged by David Angell, produced by Grub Street Production*

"The haunting fear that someone, somewhere
may be having a good time."
(describing the Puritans)

H.L. Mencken, satirist

"Give a man a fish and you feed him for a day.
Teach him how to fish and he will sit in a boat and
drink beer all day."

George Carlin, comedian

CHAPTER SEVEN

Sex

"Sex is one of the nine reasons for reincarnation. The other eight are unimportant."

Henry Miller, novelist

"Down there between our legs is, it,s like an entertainment complex in the middle of a sewage system. Who designed that ?"

Neil Tyson DeGrasse, astrophysicist

"The big difference between sex for money and sex for free is that sex for money usually costs a lot less."

Brendan Behan, novelist

"She gave me a smile I could feel in my hip pocket."

Raymond Chandler, Mystery writer

"It was a blonde, a blonde to make a Bishop kick a hole in a stained-glass window."

Raymond Chandler, writer

"Sex appeal is 50% what you've got and 50% what people think you've got."

Sophia Loren, actress

"A promiscuous person is a person who is getting more sex than you."

Victor Lownes, Playboy executive

"Good sex is like good bridge.
If you don't have a good partner,
you better have a good hand."

Mae West, actress

"Sex is like air, it's only important if you're not getting any."

"Litigation takes the place of sex at middle age."

Gore Vidal, author

"Bisexuality immediately doubles your chance for a date."

Woody Allen, Director, actor

"The last time I was inside a woman was when I went to the Statue of Liberty."

Woody Allen, Director, actor

"In my sex fantasy, nobody loves me for my mind."

Nora Eprhon, writer

"Sex at 90 is like trying to shoot pool with a piece of rope."

Camille Paglia, writer, feminist

"Every vagina is a potential landline."

Howard Stern, Radio personality

"Tumescence is the period between pubescence and senescence."

"When turkeys mate, they think of swans."

Johnny Carson, Tonight Show, host

"Absence makes the heart go yonder."

Robert Byrne

"My wife wants to have sex in the back of the car and she wants me to drive."

Rodney Dangerfield, comedian

"If it weren't for pickpockets I,d have no sex at all."

Rodney Dangerfield, comedian

"My mother never breast-fed me.
She told me she only liked me as a friend."

Rodney Dangerfield, comedian

"Everything's about sex, except sex
which is about aggression."

"I believe sex is one of the most happy, beautiful,
wholesome things money can buy."

David Lee Roth, musician

"Watching her walk down the street is like watching
two polecats in a gunny sack."

"Women should be obscene and not heard."

Groucho Marx

"Good sex depends largely on good lighting."

Oscar Wilde, playwright

"Let me shipwreck in your thighs."

Dylan Thomas, poet (from "Under Milkwood")

"I want to find the guy who created sex,
and find out what he's working on now."

James Ellroy, film noir fiction writer

"I'm straight, but not narrow-minded."

"The main reason Santa is so jolly is because he knows where all the bad girls live."

Steve Martin, comedian

"My wife is a sex object - every time I ask for sex she objects."

Les Dawson

"The difference between pornography and erotica is lighting."

Gloria Leonard

"Whoever named it necking was a poor judge of anatomy."

Groucho Marx, comedian

"If I held you any closer I'd be behind you."

Groucho Marx, comedian

"I think men talk to women so they can sleep with them and women sleep with men so they will talk to them."

Jay McInerney, author

"Outside every thin girl is a fat man trying to get in."

"Hogamus Higamus
Men are Polygamous
Higamus Hogamus
Women Monogamous"

(possibly William James, Ogden Nash, Dorothy Parker)

CHAPTER EIGHT

Alcohol

"I'd rather have a bottle in front of me than a prefrontal lobotomy."

"I'd love to have a martini, one or two at the most,
three and I'm under the table,
four and I'm under the host."

Dorothy Parker, writer, satirist

"Martini's are a lot like breasts.
One is not enough and three
are too many."

Henny Youngman, comedian

"Let me slip you out of those wet clothes
and into a dry martini."

Cole Porter, composer

"I read about the evils of drinking,
so I gave up reading."

Henry Youngman, comedian

"Work is the curse of the drinking class."

Oscar Wilde, playwright

"I never met a cold beer I didn't like."

Robert B. Parker, writer

"Alcoholism doesn't run in my family,
it practically gallops."

Michael Donahue, Boat Captain

"Twenty four hours in a day.
Twenty four cans in a case of beer.
Coincidence? I think not."

H. L. Mencken, writer, humorist

"Is life worth living? It depends on the liver."

"I drink to make other people more interesting."

Ernest Hemingway, writer

"There is nothing wrong with sobriety in moderation."

John Ciardi, poet

"I feel bad for people who don't drink, because when they wake up in the morning that's the best they're going to feel all day."

Frank Sinatra, singer, actor

"A day without wine is like a day without sunshine."

Antoine Brillat Savarin, wine connoisseur, gourmand

"Some people make spectacles of themselves
with a couple of glasses."

"Never accept a drink from a urologist."

Erma Bombeck, humorist
(her father was a urologist.)

"I drink no more than a sponge."

Rabelais, writer

" I'm not a writer with a drinking problem,
I'm a drinker with a writing problem. "

Dorothy Parker, writer, satirist

"On nights like that
every booze party ends in a fight.
Meek, little housewives feel the edge
of the carving knife
and study their husband's necks."

Raymond Carver, Mystery writer

"Either give me more wine or leave me alone."

Rumi, poet

"I drink too much. The last time I gave a urine sample it had an olive in it."

Rodney Dangerfield, comedian

"I only drink champagne on two occasions, when I'm in love and when I'm not."

Coco Chanel, fashion legend

"One tequila, two tequila, three tequila, floor."

George Carlin, comedian

"A perfect martini should be made by filling a glass with gin, waving it in the general direction of Italy."

Noel Coward, playwright, bon vivant

CHAPTER NINE

Politics

"In Washington two people can keep a secret,
but one of them has to be dead."

"If you don't vote, you don't count."

"In fact the only thing we never forgive in each other
is a difference of opinion."

Ralph Waldo Emerson, writer, philosopher

"A riddle wrapped in a mystery inside an enigma."

Winston Churchill, Prime Minister, (describing Russia)

"The root of oppression is the loss of memory."

Paula Allen Gunn, writer

"A nation of sheep will beget a
Government of wolves."

Edward R. Murrow

"You campaign in poetry, you govern in prose."

Bill Clinton, United States President

"When the speech condemns a free press,
you are hearing the words of a tyrant."

Thomas Jefferson, United States President

"If you see something is not right, not fair, not just,
you have a moral obligation
to do something about it."

John Lewis, U.S. Congressman

"Be the change you want to see in the world."

Mahatma Ghandi, spiritual leader

"We have met the enemy and he is us."

Walter Kelley, artist creator of the Pogo comic strip

"If voting could change anything,
it would be illegal."

Noam Chomsky, linguist

"It's amazing what you can accomplish
if you don't care who gets the credit."

Harry S. Truman, United States President

"History is a set of lies agreed upon."

Napoleon, emperor

"Eternal vigilance is the price of freedom."

Thomas Jefferson, United States President

"To govern is to choose between bad and worse."

John F. Kennedy, United States President

"Conflict equals exposure, exposure equals power."

Newt Gingrich, U.S. Congressman

"You can't be neutral on a moving train"

Howard Zinn, B.U. professor

"The arc of the moral universe is long,
but it tends toward justice."

Theodore Parker, Universalist minister, abolitionist

"Why talk to the horse's ass, when I can take four
steps forward talk to the horse himself."

Old Boston political saying

"Sunlight is the greatest disinfectant."

Justice Louis Brandeis, Supreme Court Justice

"Don't talk if you can whisper, Don't whisper if you can nod, Don't nod if you can wink, and try not to get caught winking."

Martin Lomasney, "The Mahatma", Boston political boss

"Now, this is not the end. It is not even the beginning of the end. But it is, perhaps the end of the beginning."

Winston Churchill, British Prime Minister

"Never waste an opportunity to use a crisis."

Rahm Emmanuel, Mayor of Chicago

"When given a choice between a Republican and a Republican, voters will always choose a Republican."

Harry S. Truman, United States President

"If I can't dance, I don't want to be part of the revolution."

Emma Goldman, revolutionary

"I never met a man I didn't like."

Will Rogers, humorist (inscribed on his headstone)

"Forgive your enemies, but never forget their names."

John F. Kennedy, United States President

"Victory has a thousand fathers and defeat is an orphan."

John F. Kennedy, United States President
(On accepting responsibility for the Bay of Pigs disaster)

"It is easier to stay out than to get out."

Mark Twain, author

"History doesn't repeat itself, but it does rhyme."

Mark Twain, author

"Unanswered questions are far less dangerous than unquestioned answers."

"Democracy is the worst form of government, except for all the rest."

Winston Churchill, former British Prime Minister

"Power tends to corrupt, and absolute power corrupts absolutely."

Lord Acton, British Parliamentarian

"A politician is a fellow who will lay down your life for his country."

Texas Guinan, actress, entrepreneur

"I think a basic principle of our constitution is nobody is above the law."

Barack Obama, United States President

"Here come the Democrats,
weaker than a Canadian hot sauce."

Jim Hightower, Texas politician, humorist

"The water won't clear
til the hogs out get out of the creek.

Jim Hightower, Texas politician, humorist

"The Democrats never miss an opportunity to miss an opportunity."

Van Jones, lawyer, television commentator

"You're entitled to your own opinion,
but you're not entitled to your own facts."

Lawrence O'Donnell, political commentator

"The first rule of economics is that there's no such thing as a free lunch."

John Kenneth Galbraith,
Nobel Prize-winning economist

"A government which robs Peter to pay Paul,
can always count on the support of Paul."

George Bernard Shaw, playwright

"If you are neutral in situations of injustice,
you have chosen the side of oppression."

Rev. Desmond Tutu, Nobel Peace Prize

"If you do not take an interest
in the affairs of your government,
then you are doomed
to live under the rule of fools."

Plato, philosopher

"Politics doesn't make strange bedfellows,
but marriage does."

Groucho Marx, comedian

"The only thing necessary for the triumph of evil is
for good men to do nothing."

Edmund Burke, philosopher

"I'm not a member of an organized political party,
I'm a Democrat."

Will Rogers, humorist, commentator

"It's not enough to change the players,
we gotta change the game."

President Barack Obama

"Democrats always find a way to snatch defeat
from the jaws of victory."

"He who controls the media,
controls the minds of the world."

Noam Chomsky, M. I. T. Linguist

"The general population doesn't know
what's happening, and it doesn't even know
that it doesn't know."

Noam Chomsky, Linguist

"When I was a boy I was told
anybody could become President;
now, I'm beginning to believe it."

Clarence Darrow, attorney

"Plutocracy and democracy don't mix."

Bill Moyers

" An adversary is not necessarily an enemy."

Richard M. Nixon, United States President

"While I detest what you say, but I will defend to my death your right to say it."

Voltaire, author

"A diplomat is a man who thinks twice before saying nothing."

Richard Gully, British aristocrat

"Diplomacy without arms is like music without instruments."

Frederick the Great

"History is the myth men choose to believe."

Napoleon

"Unanswered questions are far less dangerous than unquestioned answers."

Richard Feynman, Nobel Prize-Winning Physicist

"The beginning of the end of war lies in its remembrance."

Herman Wouk, novelist, from the "Winds of War"

"Those who can make you believe absurdities, can get you to commit atrocities."

Voltaire

CHAPTER TEN

Life and Death

"I'm not afraid of death, I just don't want to be there when it happens."

Woody Allen, comedian, director

"Dream as if you'll live forever,
live as if you'll die tomorrow."

James Dean, actor

"I'd rather reign in hell, than serve in heaven."

John Milton, poet
(quoting Lucifer in Milton's "Paradise Lost")

"The secret to life is to say yes all the time.
Because when you're old, you don't want to say:
"I wish I'd done that."

Francis Ford Coppola, director

"We are all heading to the same station."

Robert Redford, director, actor (talking about death)

"Suicide is a permanent solution
to a temporary problem."

Phil Donahue, television show host

"My work is done, why wait."

*Suicide note left by George Eastman,
founder of Eastman Kodak*

"I'm bored."

Suicide note left by George Sanders, actor

"He left friends."

epitaph on tombstone

At least tonight, I,ll know where he's sleeping."

epitaph on Key West Fl. tombstone

"I told you I was sick."

epitaph on Key West Fl. Tombstone

"I knew this was going to happen."

Dustin Hoffman, actor, musing on his future epitaph

"The unexamined life is not worth living."

Socrates, philosopher

"A life without a cause is a life without effect."

Paulo Coelho

"Life is what happens
while you're making other plans."

John Lennon, musician, songwriter

"Life should be as simple as possible,
but not simpler."

Albert Einstein, physicist, Nobel Prize winner

"Life is like riding a bicycle, in order to keep your balance, you must keep moving."

Albert Einstein, physicist, Nobel Prize winner

"Life begins beyond your comfort zone.
Live or wonder?"

Larry Flanders, Captain,
"Egret", 46' Nordhavn trawler

"I always imagined that paradise
would be a kind of library."

Jorge Luis Borges, Writer

"Life is not a spectator sport."

Jackie Robinson, Baseball Legend

"Love the people God gave you,
because He'll need them back one day."

Becky Kinder

"Life is not a dress rehearsal."

Frederick Nietzsche, philosopher

"You Don't get another chance.
Life ain't no Nintendo game."

Eminem, rapper, musician

"Life is tough, wear a helmet."

Jennifer Aniston, actress

"What we live by, we die by."

Robert Frost

"Death ends a life, not a relationship."

From "Songs I never sang for my father."

"I love walking in the rain,
because no one can see my tears."

Charlie Chaplin, director, actor

"That it will never come again
is what makes life sweet. Dwell in possibility."

Emily Dickinson

"One hour closer to death."

Lord Rothschild's clock would ring & chime this every hour, meaning, "don't waste time"

"Life is a tragedy to those who feel,
a comedy to those who think."

Horace Wallace, attorney, critic

"It seemed like a good neighborhood
to have bad habits in."

Raymond Chandler, Mystery writer

CHAPTER ELEVEN

Wealth and Money

"The wealthy are merely janitors of their possessions."

Frank Lloyd Wright, architect

"After the first million,
a hamburger still taste the same."

Bill Gates, founder of Microsoft

"We buy things we don't need,
with money we don't have,
to impress people we don't like."

Dave Ramsey, financial planner

"Being well born can save a man thirty years."

Blaise Pascal, mathematician, philosopher

"There will be no success or real reward without risk."

Robert Mayer, journalist

"The fear of death increases in exact proportion to increase in wealth."

Ernest Hemingway

"Money is a form of poetry."

Wallace Stevens, poet

"Behind every great fortune lies a great crime."

Honore de Balzac, writer

"Money doesn't talk, it swears."

Bob Dylan, songwriter, performer

"Money talks and bullshit walks,"

Mickey "Ozzie" Myers, U.S. Congressman, convicted tax felon

"The rich are different."

F. Scott Fitzgerald

"Yeah, they have more money."

Ernest Hemingway, Wealth and Money

"An imbalance between the rich and the poor is one of the oldest and most fatal ailments of all republics."

Plutarch, historian

"If you're poor you're crazy.
If you're rich you're eccentric."

"Cash combined with courage in a time of crisis is priceless."

Warren Buffet, investor

"Only the little people pay taxes."

Leona Helmsley, "Queen of Mean", convicted tax felon

"I'd like to live like a poor person, only with lots of money."

Pablo Picasso, artist

"The rich aren't like us, they pay less taxes."

Peter DeVries, novelist

"It's like standing in a cold shower, tearing up thousand dollar bills."

Ted Turner, Entrepreneur, describing financing an America's Cup Yacht

"Poor George, he was born on third base and he thought he hit a triple."

Ann Richards, Texas Governor describing George W. Bush

"Poor George, he was born with a silver foot in his mouth."

Ann Richards, Texas Governor describing George W. Bush

"There are people who have money, and then there are people who are rich."

Coco Chanel, fashion icon

"I've been broke, but I've never been poor."

Mike Todd, movie producer

"The wretchedness of being rich is that you live with rich people."

Logan Pearsall Smith, writer

"I'd rather be smart and poor, than rich and dumb."

Ted Turner, CNN founder

"We weren't poor. We were Po'. We were so poor, we couldn't afford the other O and R."

Erica J. Suter, lawyer

"Money changes everything."

Cyndi Lauper, musician, songwriter

"Rich people have small TVs and big libraries and poor people have large TVs and small libraries."

Zig Ziglar, motivational speaker

"The poor wish to be rich,
the rich wish to be happy.
The single wish to be married,
the married wish to be dead."

Ann Landers, advice columnist

"Money can't buy you happiness,
but it can buy you a yacht big enough
to pull up right next to it."

David Lee Roth, rock musician

"Money can't buy you happiness,
but it can buy you a better class of enemies."

Spike Milligan, entertainer

"After a rich man gets rich,
his next ambition is to get richer."

"As they say in Palm Beach,
you can never be too rich or too thin."

"If you can count your money,
you're not a billionaire."

J. Paul Getty, billionaire

"A fool and his money are soon parted."

"A fool and his money are soon invited everywhere."

Warren Buffet, billionaire investor

"A fool and his money are soon married."

Carolyn Wells

"A fool and his money are soon elected."

Will Rogers, humorist

"A fool and his money are soon partying."

Steven Wright, comedian

"Decadence is opulence with an expiration date."

F. Scott Fitzgerald

"Money is the root of all evil."

"The lack of money is the root of all evil."

Mark Twain, author, raconteur

"Anybody who tells you money is the root of all evil, doesn't have any."

Ben Affleck, actor, director

"If you want to know what God thinks of money, just look at the people he gave it to."

Dorothy Parker

"A truly rich man is one whose children run into his arms when his hands are empty."

"A sunny place for shady people."

Somerset Maugham, novelist,
describing the French Riviera

"The Lucky Sperm Club: They make money the old fashioned way, they inherit it."

"Be careful to leave your sons well instructed
rather than rich.
For those well instructed
are better than the wealth of the ignorant."

Epictetus, philosopher

"If at first you don't succeed, take the tax loss."

Kirk Kirkpatrick, Businessman

"A rich man is nothing
but a poor man with money."

W.C. Fields, comedian

"The rich get richer, the poor get children."

F. Scott Fitzgerald, novelist

Get rich, or die trying."

Curtis Jackson, rapper, also known as "50 cent"

"A bull market is like sex.
It feels best just before it ends."

Warren Buffet, investor

"Even the rich are hungry for love, for being cared for, for being wanted, for having someone all to their own."

Mother Teresa

"My philosophy has always been, do what you love and the money will follow."

Amy Weber, actress

"Rich people stay rich by living like they're broke.
Broke people stay broke by living like they're rich."

"No man is rich enough to buy back his past."

Oscar Wilde, playwright

"The sly, sharp instinct for self-preservation that passes for wisdom among the rich."

Evelyn Waugh, author

CHAPTER TWELVE

On Growing Old

"I don't want to die feeling I never lived."

Henry David Thoreau

"A beautiful face will age, and a perfect body will change, but a beautiful soul will always be a beautiful soul."

"The farther one goes, the less ones knows."

Tao Te Ching, philosopher

"Enjoy the little things in life.... because one day you'll look back and realize they were the big things."

Kurt Vonnegut, novelist

"Because I don't let the Old Man in."

Clint Eastwood, actor, director, when asked how he maintains his vitality and physical prowess

"In the depths of winter I found within myself an eternal summer."

Albert Camus, Nobel Prize winner in Literature

"Be ashamed to die until you've had a victory for humanity."

Horace Mann, educational reformer, U.S. Congressman

"Be here, now."

Baba Ram Dass, Harvard professor, spiritual leader

"What I hear I forget, what I see I remember, what I do I understand."

"If youth only knew, if age only could."

George Bernard Shaw, playwright

"Being 70 is not a sin. It's not a joke either."

Golda Meir, Former Israeli Prime Minister

"Talk about your blessings
more than you talk about your problems."

"We live alone, we die alone, everything else
is just an illusion."

Orson Welles, Director, actor

"I mourn the life I'm living."

Anton Checkov, writer

"Retirement must be wonderful. I mean you can only suck in your stomach for so long."

Burt Reynolds, actor

"And the crack in the tea-cup opens a lane to the land of the dead."

W. H. Auden, poet

"Our pursuit of youth blinds us to the possibility of age."

Ralph Waldo Emerson, poet, transcendentalist

"Beautiful young people are accidents of nature, but beautiful old people are works of art."

"The age of a woman doesn't mean a thing. The best tunes are played on the oldest fiddles."

"The older the violin, the better the music."

"A man's face is his autobiography. A woman's face is her work of fiction."

Oscar Wilde, writer, playwright

"The problem with beauty is that it's like being born rich and getting poor."

Joan Collins, actress

"Don't ruin a good day today by thinking about a bad day yesterday."

"To lengthen thy life, lessen thy meals."

Ben Franklin

"I used to worry about how people looked at me. Now I worry about how I look at them."

Brooke Astor, 100 yr old NY socialite

"It takes a long time to grow an old friend."

John Leonard, critic

"Life is more than just maintaining oneself,
it's about extending oneself.
Otherwise life is only not dying."

Simone de Beauvoir, writer, feminist

"You will know you're old
when you ceased to be amazed."

Noel Coward, playwright, bon vivant

"The old believe everything, the middle-aged suspect everything. The young know everything."

"A woman is as old she looks,
a man is old if he stops looking."

Iris Apfel, Fashion icon

"Wrinkles should only indicate
where the smiles have been."

Mark Twain, author, raconteur

"Know the child and you know the adult."

"As a man grows older, he should keep his
friendships in good repair."

Ben Johnson, writer

"If youth only knew, if age only could."

Henri Estienne, French scholar

"Growing old is not for sissies."

Bette Davis, actress

"Youth is such a wonderful thing. What a crime it is to waste it on the young."

George Bernard Shaw, playwright

CHAPTER THIRTEEN

Intelligence and Genius

"The difference between genius and stupidity is, genius has it's limits."

Albert Einstein, Nobel Prize winning physicist

"The ability to hold two competing thoughts in one's mind and still be able to function is the mark of the superior mind."

F. Scott Fitzgerald, novelist

"Genius is infinite patience."

Michaelangelo, artist

"You cannot think about thinking
without thinking about something."

Seymour Paper, M.I.T. Professor

"Perspective is worth 50 points of an IQ."

Alan Kay, Apple Computer

"Passion is the genesis of genius."

Galileo, astronomer

"Music is the effort we make to explain
how our brains work."

Dr. Lewis Thomas

"If you can't explain it simply,
you don't understand it well enough."

Albert Einstein, Nobel Prize winning physicist

"The United States was founded
by the brightest people in the country
and we haven't seen them since."

Gore Vidal, writer

"The mind is like an iceberg.
It floats with one-seventh of it's bulk is above water."

Sigmund Freud, psychiatrist

"Some people drink from the fountain of knowledge
others just gargle."

"Knowledge is power."

Sir Francis Bacon, philosopher

"I choose a lazy person to do a hard job, because a
lazy person will find an easy way to do it."

Bill Gates, founder, Microsoft

"Genius may be the ability to say a profound thing in a simple way."

Charles Bukowski, poet

"Acquaint yourself with your own ignorance."

Isaac Watts, autodidact,
(from "Improvements of the mind")

"The man who doesn't read books has no advantage over the man who can't read."

Mark Twain, writer, raconteur

"When in doubt, look intelligent."

Garrison Keillor, writer

"Knowing how to think empowers you far beyond those who only know what to think."

Neil Tyson deGrasse, astrophysicist

"If a machine is expected to be infallible,
it cannot also be intelligent."

Alan Turing, computer scientist

"A man provided with a pencil, paper, and rubber
and subject to strict discipline is in effect,
a universal machine."

Alan Turing, computer scientist

"I don't care that they stole my idea.
I care that they don't have any ideas of their own."

Nikola Tesla, inventor

"Half of the American people have never read a
newspaper. Half have never voted for President.
One hopes it is the same half."

Gore Vidal, author

"I think this is the most extraordinary collection of talent, of human knowledge, that has ever been gathered at the White House, with the possible exception of when Thomas Jefferson dined alone."

President John F. Kennedy, Speaking at a State dinner honoring Nobel Prize recipients

"When a true genius appears you will know him by this sign. That the dunces are in a confederacy against him."

Jonathan Swift, author

"You can always tell a Harvard man,
You just can't tell him much."

CHAPTER FOURTEEN

Perseverance

"Our greatest glory is not in never failing, but in rising every time we fail."

Confucius

"Success is the ability to go from one failure to another with no loss of enthusiasm."

Winston Churchill, Prime Minister

"The obstacles in your path are not obstacles. They are the path."

Jane Lotter, author

"Ninety percent of life, is showing up."

Woody Allen, writer, director

"Inspiration is for amateurs.
The rest of us just show up for work."

Chuck Close, writer

"The beginning is the most important part of work."

Plato, philosopher

"Invention is 1% inspiration
and 99 % perspiration."

Thomas Edison, inventor
"Edison failed 10,000 times
before he made the electric light bulb."

Do not be discouraged if you fail a few times."

Napoleon Hill, author, motivational speaker

"Hardships often prepare ordinary people for an extraordinary destiny."

"There are no traffic jams along the extra mile."

Roger Staubach, football player, Heisman trophy winner

"If you can't fly, then run, if you can't run,
then walk. If you can't walk, then crawl,
by all means keep moving."

Martin Luther King Jr.

"It's no use saying, we are doing our best...
It is only important to do what is necessary."

Winston Churchill, British Prime Minister

"Ideas are a dime a dozen.
People who put them in action are priceless."

Mary Kay Ash, Cosmetics pioneer

"Thankfully, persistence is a great substitute
for talent."

Steve Martin, entertainer, comedian

"Vision without execution is hallucination."

Walter Isaacson, biographer

"There,s only the trying, again and again."

T. S. Eliot, poet

"The world is run by those who show up"

Robert Johnson, entrepreneur

"I found a book entitled:
"How to be amazing at anything,
It had a single page,
It had a single word - Practice."

"How do you to get to Carnegie Hall?
Practice, practice, practice."

"Success consists of a series of little daily victories."

Laddie F. Hutar, management consultant

"When times get tough, we don't give up, we get up."

President Barack Obama

CHAPTER FIFTEEN

Silence

"Silence is the most perfect expression of scorn."

George Bernard Shaw, playwright

"The word listen contains the same letters as the word silent."

"Silence is a true friend who never betrays."

Confucius, philosopher

"Don't solve her problems,
she simply wants your attention,
keep your mouth shut."

"Think a lot, say little, write nothing."

J. Pierpont Morgan, financier

"Never miss a good chance to just shut up."

Will Rogers, humorist

"If you are too tired to speak, sit next to me, because I too am fluent in silence."

"Listening often is the only thing needed to help someone."

"When you're right, be quiet."

Deeksha Josh

"Never assume that loud is strong and quiet is weak."

"Listen to silence, it has much to say."

Rumi, poet

"It takes a great man to be a good listener."

Arthur Helpers, author

"Let thy speech be better than silence or be silent."

Dionysius of Carnasuss

"Learn to get in touch
with the silence within yourself
and know that everything in life has purpose."

Elizabeth Kubler-Ross, author, "On Death and Dying"

"Silence is not the absence of something,
but the presence of everything."

Gordon Hemphill, Business Consultant

"When you talk, you are only repeating what you already know. But when you listen you may learn something new."

Dalai Lama

"Only in a quiet mind is there adequate perception of the universe."

Hans Marlois

"Oppression can only survive through silence."

Carmen de Monteflores, singer, songwriter

"In the end, we will not remember the words of our enemies, but the silence of our friends."

Martin Luther King Jr., spiritual leader

"Saying nothing sometimes says the most."

Emily Dickinson, poet

" As my father told me, never write it down."

Robert F. Kennedy
(speaking to CIA Director John McClone)

"In the attitude of silence the soul finds
the path in a clearer light,
and what is elusive and deceptive
reveals itself in crystal clearness."

Mahatma Ghandi

"The cruelest lies are often told in silence."

Robert Louis Stevenson, author

"Not merely an absence of noise, real silence begins
when a reasonable being withdraws
from the noise to find peace and order
in his inner sanctuary."

Peter Minard, writer

"When thought of as a fool,
sometimes it is better to remain silent
than to speak up
and remove all doubt."

Abraham Lincoln, United States President

"Breathing in I calm my body and mind. Breathing out, I smile, dwelling in the present moment."

Thich Nhat Hahn, spiritual leader

CHAPTER SIXTEEN

On Writing

"Writing is easy. Just sit in front of a typewriter, open a vein and bleed it out drop by drop."

Red Smith, columnist

"If you get up every morning and write a page before you pee, in 365 days, you'll have written a novel."

Charles Willeford, mystery writer

"Childhood is the bank balance of the writer."

Graham Greene, author

"The willing suspension of disbelief."

Samuel Taylor Coleridge,
writer, describing fiction writing

"Writing is the art of applying the ass to the seat."

Dorothy Parker, satirist

"Income tax returns are the most imaginative fiction being written today."

Herman Wouk, author

"Subvert the dominant paradigm."

Virginia Woolf

"If one wants to write, one simply has to organize one's life into a mass of little habits."

Graham Greene

"I work until beer o'clock."

Stephen King

"I used to be treated like an idiot, now I'm treated like an idiot-Savant."

Martin Cruz Smith, after his novel "Gorky Park" became a Best-seller

"His prose has all the sparkle of a second mortgage."

Dick Cavett, talk show host

"I am in the smallest room in my house.
Your review is before me.
Very soon it will be behind me."

George Bernard Shaw,
responding to a Critic's review of his play.

"You can't wait for inspiration.
You have to go after it with a club."

Jack London

"First, you clean your refrigerator."

Ernest Hemingway, when asked how to write a novel

"The first draft of everything is Shit."

Ernest Hemingway, author

"The writer dies twice: once when the body dies, and once when the talent dies."

Martin Amis, writer

"If only I had more time, I would have written a shorter letter."

Blaise Pascal, writer

"Boy meets girl; girl gets boy into pickle. Boy gets pickle into girl."

Jack Woodford, describing the structure of a novel

"If you own the story, you get to write the story."

Brene Brown, writer, motivational speaker

"Write something, even if it's a suicide note."

Gore Vidal

"Writing a novel is like driving at night in the fog.
You can only see as far as your headlights,
but in doing so you can go the whole way.
That's the way I write.
I don't know what's next."

E.L. Doctorow, author

"Show me a hero and I'll write you a tragedy."

F. Scott Fitzgerald, author

"Never underestimate the power of funny,
it moves mountains."

James Patterson, author

"It took him only twelve lines to say
what it took me a book to write."

John Steinbeck, Woody Guthrie's song
"This land is your land."

"Keep a sense of humor,
try to be as intelligent as possible,
but don't take life too seriously."

Wendy Wasserstein, playwright

"Just start at page one
and write like a son of a bitch."

Jim Harrison, author "Legends of the Fall."

"If you steal from one author its plagiarism.
If you steal from many it's research."

Wilson Mizner, writer

"Boston is a place without springboards
for people who can't dive."

E. E. Cummings, poet, to writer, John Cheever,
why he should leave Boston

"Never mistake motion for action."

Ernest Hemingway, author

"I think like a genius, I write like a distinguished
author, I speak like a child."

Vladimir Nabokov, author

"To be a poet is a condition, not a profession."

Robert Frost, poet

"I had a lover's quarrel with the world."

Inscribed on Robert Frost's tombstone

"Be violent and disturbed in your fiction,
so you can be gentle and normal in your life."

Gustave Flaubert

"In order to be a good writer you must have
an absolutely, infallible, built-in bullshit, detector."

Ernest Hemingway,

"If there is a book you want to read
and it isn't written, Write it."

Shel Silverstein, writer

CHAPTER SEVENTEEN

Men and Women

"Once you've seen a woman take her bra off without removing her shirt, it makes more sense why women should be in charge of everything.

"If men could get pregnant, abortion would be a sacrament."

Woman cabdriver in Boston, speaking to feminist, Flo Kennedy

"Men are afraid women will laugh at them. Women are afraid men will kill them."

Margaret Atwood

"A man who cooks is attractive. A man who does the dishes is irresistible."

"To find out a girl's faults, praise her to her friends."

Ben Franklin

"Mothers are far fonder than fathers of their children because they are more certain they are their own."

Aristotle

"Hurricanes are a lot like women;
when they come they're wet and wild,
but when they leave
they take your house and car."

"Men and ships rot in port."

Oscar Wilde, playwright

"God gave all men a penis and a brain,
but only enough blood
to run one at a time."

Robin Williams, comedian

"Women are either at your feet or at your throat."

Winston Churchill, British Prime Minister

"The ideal husband understands every word
his wife doesn't say."

Alfred Hitchcock

"Listen to the woman when she looks at you,
not when she talks to you."

Kahlil Gibran, philosopher

"A woman without a man
is like a fish without a bicycle."

graffiti on the restroom wall
of a Harvard Square restaurant

"I'm a marvelous housekeeper.
Every time I leave a man I take his house."

Zsa Zsa Gabor, actress

"Husbands are like fires -
They go out when unattended."

Zsa Zsa Gabor

"It's never as easy to keep your own spouse happy as it is to make someone else's husband happy."

Zsa Zsa Gabor

"A male gynecologist is like an auto mechanic who has never owned a car."

Carrie Snow, comedienne

"It is impossible for a man to learn what he thinks he already knows."

Epictetus, philosopher

"A secretary must think like a man, act like a lady, look like a girl and work like a dog."

CHAPTER EIGHTEEN

Sports Quotes

"Sports is simply life with the volume turned up."

Joan Cronan, sportswriter

"The secret of managing in baseball is to keep the five guys who hate you away from the four guys who are undecided."

Casey Stengel, Legendary NY Yankees Baseball Manager

"Well, I worked for him
before and after he was a genius."

Warren Spahn, baseball Hall of Fame pitcher,
describing his Playing for Baseball legend Casey Stengel

"Don't give up, Don't ever give up."

Jim Valvano, North Carolina State basketball coach

"When you win, say nothing.
When you lose, say less."

Paul Brown, Cleveland Browns

"You miss 100 % of the shots you don't take."

Wayne Gretzky, Hockey Legend,
(on why he took so many shots)

"You were born to be a player.
You were meant to be here.
This moment is yours."

Herb Brooks, 1980 USA Olympic Hockey Coach addressing his team just before facing the undefeated Russians at Lake Placid.

"Push yourself again and again.
Don't stop until the buzzer rings."

Larry Bird, Boston Celtics Basketball Legend

"Hurting people is my business."

Sugar Ray Robinson,
World Middleweight Boxing Champion

"Everyone has a plan
until they get punched in the mouth."

Mike Tyson, World Heavyweight Champion."

"Float like a butterfly sting like a bee."

Muhammed Ali,
World Heavyweight Boxing Champion

"You can't win until you learn how to learn.

Kareem Abdul-Jabbar, L. A. Laker basketball legend.

"When you get to the end zone,
act like you,ve been there before."

attributed to many sources, including Paul Brown, Vince Lombardi, Lou Holz and "Bear" Bryant

"If I knew I was going to live this long,
I'd have taken better care of myself."

Mickey Mantle, NY Baseball Legend

"Ninety percent of baseball is half mental."

Yogi Berra, NY Yankee Baseball Legend

"If people don't want to come to the ballpark,
nobody's going to stop them."

Yogi Berra, NY Yankee

"He hits from both sides of the plate.
He's amphibious."

Yogi Berra, NY Yankee

"Cricket is basically baseball on Valium."

Robin Williams, comedian

CHAPTER NINETEEN

The Sea

"The sea finds out everything you did wrong."

Francis Stokes, writer, sailor

"Sailing is a lot like sex. Even when its bad,
its still pretty good."

Roger Crawford, Boatbuilder

"Be the calm person in the boat."

Thich Nhat Hahn, poet, Zen Master

"Attitude is the difference between
an ordeal and an adventure."

Bob Bitchin, author, Publisher,
Latitudes and Attitudes,magazine

"If you can't tie a knot, tie a lot."

"There is nothing quite so good as a burial at sea.
It is simple, tidy and not very incriminating."

Alfred Hitchcock, Director

"Why join the Navy if you can be a pirate."

Steve Jobs, founder, Apple Computer

"Twenty years from now you will be more disappointed by the things you didn't do than the things you did do. So throw off the bowlines. Catch the trade winds in your sails. Explore. Dream. Discover."

Mark Twain, author, raconteur

"The pessimist complains about the wind;
the optimist expects it to change;
the realist adjusts the sails."

William Arthur Ward, writer

"Sailing unties the knots in my mind."

Al Noble, sailor

"He who is staring at the sea is already sailing."

Paul Carver, sailor

"The only way to get a good crew is to marry one."

Eric Hiscock, sailor, author

"Hardships often prepare ordinary people
for an extraordinary destiny."

from the "Voyage of the Dawn Treader"

"Only in quiet waters
things mirror themselves undistorted."

"Life is a shipwreck,
but we must not forget to sing in the lifeboats."

Voltaire, author "

"There are only two colors to paint a boat,
black or white. Anyone who paints their boat black is
a damn fool."

L. Francis Herreshoff, Yacht Designer

"A smooth sea never made a skilled mariner."

English proverb

"They sicken of the calm, who knew the storm."

Dorothy Parker, author, satirist

"The cure for everything is salt water."

Isaak Dinesen, author

"The snot green, scrotum-tightening sea."

excerpt from the James Joyce novel "Ulysses"

"Meditation, it's not what you think.
Thought is like the waves on the ocean.
Meditation is the ocean."

Jon Kabatt-Zinn, Physician, Meditation Pioneer

"Only two sailors, in my experience,
never ran aground. One never left port,
and the other was a notorious liar."

Don Bamford, sailor

"Beware of small leaks,
a small one can sink a great ship."

Ben Franklin

"Remember, therapy is a boat to get you across the river, but most people don't want to get out."

Dr. Helen Myss, psychotherapist

"If you spend a night alone in an open boat in a thunderstorm, it will bring you closer to God than going to church for forty Sunday's."

L. Francis Herreshoff, nautical architect

"The sea does not reward those who are too anxious, too green or too impatient."

"Blue, green, grey, white or black: smooth, ruffled, or mountainous; the ocean is not silent."

H. P. Lovecraft, writer

CHAPTER TWENTY

Proverbs

"Don't cry over spilt milk,
it could have been whiskey."

Irish proverb

"Happy wife, happy life."

Asian proverb

"Examine what is said, not him who speaks."

Arab proverb

"A patient woman can roast an ox with a lantern."

Chinese proverb

"There is no solution, seek it lovingly."

Zen proverb

"Knows the way, stops seeing."

Korean proverb

"Trust in God, but tie your camel."

Arab proverb

"Precision of thought, economy of expression."

Dr. Anthony Fauci, CDC spokesman,
quoting Jesuit proverb

"Truth is always encountered but rarely perceived."

Zen proverb

"As the twig is bent, so grows the tree."

Alexander Pope, poet

"This too shall pass."

Persian adage

"He couldn't hit a bull in the ass
with a handful of rice."

Southern saying

"All hat and no cattle."

Texas proverb

"All po' and no mo."

Texas proverb (all potential and no momentum)

"The guest is the donkey of the host."

Turkish proverb

"The milk of the sacred cow
has a way of turning sour."

Hindu proverb

"If their is no wind, row."

Latin proverb

"A lawyer and his wagon must be well greased."

German proverb

"Fall seven times and stand up eight."

Japanese proverb

"If you want your ship to come in,
you must build a dock."

Maritime proverb

"Truth is the daughter of time."

English proverb, attributed to Francis Bacon

"If a frog had wings he wouldn't bump his booty."

Jimy Williams, former Red Sox manager

"Shut my mouth and shine my shoes."

Southern saying

"If it moves salute it, if it doesn't paint it."

U. S. Navy mantra

"If someone is buttering you up,
they're probably planning on taking a bite."

country proverb

"Don't get mad, get even."

South Boston saying

"If you say anything, say nothing."

South Boston saying

"Like bells they hang together."

English proverb

"It's hard tellin', not Knowin'"

Maine saying

"You can't get there from here."

Maine saying

"I'm as busy as a one-legged guy
in an ass-kicking contest."

Country saying

"The secret to living well and longer is: eat half, walk double, laugh triple and love without measure."

Tibetan proverb

"It's not the size of the dog in the fight, but rather the fight in the dog."

Proverb attributed to Mark Twain

"Tell your friend a lie, if he keeps it a secret, then tell him the truth."

Portuguese Proverb

"No one starts out as a cow thief, they start out as a needle thief."

Mi Sun's Grandmother (Korean proverb)

"The learning is in the doing."

Lakota saying

CHAPTER TWENTY ONE

Foreign Language Quotes

"Dolce Far niente"

Italian. English translation:
"The sweetness of doing nothing."

"Lux Omni vincit

Latin. English translation: "Light conquers all."

Ancora imparo "

Italian. English translation: "I'm still learning,"
attributed to Michelangelo

"Sic semper tyrannus."

Latin. English translation:
"Thus always to tyrants", John Wilkes Booth

"No lite te bastardes carborundum"

Latin. English translation:
"Don't let the bastards wear you down."

"Non impediti ratione cogitationis"

Latin translation: "Unencumbered by thought."
attributed to Click and Clack,
Ray and Tom Magliozzi, NPR

"Amor Omni vincit."

Latin translation: "Love conquers all."

"Quo praebet university."

Latin. English translation: "The universe provides."

"Sic transit gloria mundi."

Latin. English translation:
"Thus passes the glory of the world."

"Hara hachi bu."

Japanese. English translation:
Japanese theory of only eating til you're two-thirds full.

"Cum dubito desisto."

Latin. English translation: "When in doubt, don't."
referenced by Dame Maggie Smith,
actress when asked for life advice.

"Vivre sans aimer n'est pas proprement vivre."

French. English translation:
"To live without loving is not to live."

"Noli timere."

Latin. English translation: "Do not be afraid."
Seamus Heaney, Nobel Prize in Poetry

"Parvus sed potens."

Latin. English translation: "Small but powerful."

"Fortis in arduis"

Latin. English translation: "Brave in difficulties."

"Scientia Potentia Est"

Latin, English translation: "Knowledge is Power"

CHAPTER TWENTY TWO

Fashion and Style

"People will stare, make it worth their while."

Bill Blass, Fashion Icon

"Simplicity is the ultimate sophistication."

Leonardo da Vinci

"Fashion is the armor to survive everyday life."

Bill Cunningham, NY Times fashion photographer

"One is never underdressed or overdressed in a little black dress."

Karl Lagerfeld, Fashion Director, Chanel

"Imperfection is fine."

Anna Wintour, editor, Vogue Magazine

"I have the simplest of taste. I am always satisfied with the best."

Oscar Wilde, playwright

"When planning to travel, take out all your clothes and all your money, then take half your clothes and all of your money."

Diana Vreeland, editor Vogue Magazine

"Fashion may go out of style,
but style will never go out of fashion."

Coco Chanel, Fashion Icon

"I never dreamed about success, I worked for it."

Estée Lauder, Cosmetics entrepreneur

CHAPTER TWENTY THREE

Art and Culture

"Good artists copy, great artists steal."

Pablo Picasso, Artist

"Show me a man who works with his hands and I'll show you a laborer. Show me a man who works with his hands and his mind and I'll show you a craftsman. Show me a man who works with his hands, his mind and his heart and I'll show you an artist."

"There's no such thing as simple. Simple is hard."

Martin Scorsese, Director

"No great work of art is ever finished."

Michelangelo

"Art isn't chaste. If it's chaste it isn't, art."

Pablo Picasso, Artist

"An artist's studio should be a small space, because small rooms discipline the mind and large ones distract it."

Leonardo da Vinci

"There is peace even in the storm."

Vincent Van Gogh

"I am always doing that which I cannot do, in order that I may learn to do it."

Pablo Picasso

"When I say artist, I mean the man who is building things.... some with a brush - some with a shovel- some choose a pen."

Jackson Pollock

"We have to change to remain the same."

Willem DeKooning

"It took me four years to paint like Raphael,
but a lifetime to paint like a child."

Pablo Picasso

"Creativity takes a wild mind and a disciplined eye."

Dorothy Parker

"An essential aspect of creativity is
not being afraid to fail."

Dr. Edwin Land, founder, Polaroid Corporation

CHAPTER TWENTY FOUR

Celebrity and Movie Quotes

"I didn't say half the things I said."

Yogi Berra

"Inside every cynical person,
there is a disappointed idealist."

George Carlin

"Two wrongs don't make a right, but three lefts do."

Oscar Wilde, playwright

"Is this chicken or fish ?"

Jessica Simpson,
while eating a Chicken of the Sea tuna sandwich

"Before you judge a man, walk a mile in his shoes. After that who cares? He's a mile away and you've got his shoes."

Billy Connolly

"Have you noticed that all the people in favor of birth control are already born."

Benny Hill

"Some people know the price of everything and the value of nothing."

Oscar Wilde

"If all the girls who attended the Yale prom were laid end to end, I wouldn't be a bit surprised."

Dorothy Parker

"If Love is blind, why is lingerie so popular?"

Dorothy Parker

"Of course I talk to myself. I like a good speaker, and I appreciate an intelligent audience."

Dorothy Parker

"This is not a novel to be tossed aside lightly. It should be thrown with great force."

Dorothy Parker

"Ducking for apples - change one letter and it's the story of my life."

Dorothy Parker

"You can take a horse to water, but you can't make him drink. You can take a whore to culture, but you can't make her think."

Dorothy Parker,
addressing the American Horticultural Society

"She got her looks from her father -
he's a plastic surgeon."

Groucho Marx

"Military justice is to justice
as military music is to music."

Groucho Marx

"Military intelligence is a contradiction in terms."

Groucho Marx

"Who are you going to believe
me or your lying eyes?"

Chico Marx, from the 1933 movie, "Duck Soup"

"Either he's dead or my watch has stopped."

Groucho Marx, from the 1937 movie,
"A day at the races."

"I never forget a face, but in your case,
I'll make an exception."

Groucho Marx, comedian

"Why a four-year old could understand this report.
Run out and find me a four-year old child."

Groucho Marx, from the 1933, movie, "Duck Soup"

"I refuse to join any club that would accept me
as one of its members."

Groucho Marx,

"I'm only half-Jewish, can I go into the pool
up to my waist?"

Groucho Marx, on not being allowed entry into a restricted country club pool

---

"You can have anything you want in life,
you just can't have everything you want in life."

Ray Dalio, founder, Bridgewater Associates hedge fund

"Consistency is the hobgoblin of shallow minds."

Oscar Wilde

"Patriotism is the last refuge of scoundrels"

Oscar Wilde

"A thing is not necessarily true
because a man died for it."

Oscar Wilde

"No man is rich enough to buy back his past."

Oscar Wilde

"I'm not young enough to know everything."

Oscar Wilde

"Three chords and the truth."

Willie Nelson, songwriter, musician, describing country music.

"It's beauty which captures your attention, personality which captures your heart."

Oscar Wilde

"Always forgive your enemies, nothing annoys them so much."

Oscar Wilde

"The only way to get rid of temptation is to give in to it."

Oscar Wilde

"Hypocrisy is the compliment vice pays to virtue."

Oscar Wilde

"I went from nothing, to something, to everything."

Conor McGregor, Mixed Martial Arts World Champion

"Sunny with patches of envy,
and a good chance of schadenfrude."

Bruce Feinstein, Vanity Fair, (describing L.A.)

"Tread softly, because you tread on my dreams."

William Butler Yeats

"Tell me who you walk with
and I'll tell you who you are."

Miguel Cervantes

"You are entering into a dimension not only of sight and sound, but a journey into a wondrous land of imagination. Next stop, The Twilight Zone."

Rod Serling, host, "The Twilight Zone."

"Stick with me kid,
and you'll be farting through silk."

Robert Mitchum, actor, talking to his wife

"I must go home periodically
to renew my sense of horror."

Carson McCullers

"The hottest place in hell is reserved for those who in a time of moral crisis maintain their neutrality."

Dante Alighieri, Dante's Inferno

"A lawsuit is the suicide of time."

Thomas Edison

"We do survive every moment after all,
except the last one."

John Updike

"There are decades where nothing happens and there are weeks where decades happen."

Vladimir Lenin

"I eat NO for breakfast."

Vice President Kamala Harris,
first African-Asian American V. P.

"The ability to observe without evaluating is the highest form of intelligence."

Krishnamurti

"Bad taste creates more millionaires than good taste."

Charles Bukowski, poet

"I'm so broke, I can't even pay attention."

Tom Waits, singer

"Money in Bermuda disappears as fast as an ice cube on a black-top road at high noon in the tropics."

Donald Street, editor, Cruising World Magazine

"If only I had a little more humility, I'd be perfect."

Ted Turner, CNN founder

"Magicians are only as good as their last illusion."

Richard Goodwin, JFK speechwriter

"It's like being nibbled to death by a duck."

Eric Sevareid, CBS newscaster,
describing dealing with network executives.

"The secret to success is to do the common thing uncommonly well."

John D. Rockefeller Jr.

"Nothing is impossible, the word itself says, I'm possible."

Audrey Hepburn

"I began by acting like the person I wanted to be, and eventually I became that person."

Cary Grant, actor

"An actor is a guy who if you ain't talking about him, he ain't listening."

Marlon Brando

"I think your whole life shows in your face and you should be proud of that."

Lauren Bacall

"Any man who goes to a psychiatrist ought to have his head examined."

Samuel Goldwyn, movie mogul

"An oral contract isn't worth
the paper it's written on."

Samuel Goldwyn

"Give me a smart idiot over a stupid genius."

Samuel Goldwyn

"I'll give you a definite maybe."

Samuel Goldwyn

"Let's have some new cliches."

Samuel Goldwyn

"I had a monumental idea this morning,
but I didn't like it."

Samuel Goldwyn

"Passion is the enemy of precision."

Darryl Zero,

"If you're a bird, be an early bird.
But If you're a worm, sleep late."

Shel Silverstein

"Don't discuss your dreams. Pursue them!"

Sylvester Stallone

"Going in one more round
when you don't think you can
that's what makes all the difference in your life."

Sylvester Stallone

"The best pilots fly more than the others;
that's why they're the best."

Chuck Yeager,
Test pilot, broke the sound barrier, Mach 1

"He was swayed by the pescadile influence."

Red Smith, L. A. Times Sports Columniston Fly-fishing

"I always read the last page of a book first, so that if I die before I finish it, I'll know how it turned out."

Nora Ephron

"It's like deja vu all over again."

Yogi Berra

"The future ain't what it used to be."

Yogi Berra

"You can observe a lot just by watching."

Yogi Berra

"Always go to other people's funerals,
otherwise they won't go to yours."

Yogi Berra

"You better cut that pizza into four slices,
because I'm not hungry enough to eat six slices."

Yogi Berra

"I didn't say half the things I said."

Yogi Berra

"Fasten your seatbelts.
It's going to be a bumpy night."

Bette Davis, "All about Eve"
film, directed by Joseph Mankiewicz,
United States, produced by Darryl Zanuck, 1950

"My name is Inigo Montoya. You killed my father. Prepare to die."

Mandy Patinkin, "Princess Bride"
film, directed by Rob Reiner
United States, produced by Rob Reiner &
Andrew Scheinman, 1987

"I'm going to make him an offer he can't refuse."

Marlon Brando, "The Godfather" film,
directed by Francis Ford Coppola,
United States, produced by Albert Ruddy, 1972

"Leave the gun, take the cannoli."

James Caan, "The Godfather"
film, directed by Francis Ford Coppola,
United States, produced by Albert Ruddy, 1972

"Keep your friends close, but keep your enemies closer.

Al Pacino, "The Godfather, Part II",
film, directed by Francis Ford Coppola,
United States, produced by Francis Ford Coppola, 1974

"What we've got here is failure to communicate."

Paul Newman, "Cool Hand Luke",
film, directed by Stuart Rosenberg,
United States, produced by Gordon Carroll, 1967

"I'll have what she's having."

Estelle Reiner, " When Harry met Sally",
film, directed by Rob Reiner,
United States, produced by Rob Reiner &
Andrew Scheinman, 1989

"Say hello to my little friend."

Al Pacino, "Scarface",
film, directed by Brian DePalma,
United States, produced by Martin Bergman, 1983

"I'll be back."

Arnold Schwarzenegger, in "Terminator",
film, directed by James Cameron,
United States, produced by Gale Ann Hurd, 1984

"You're going to need a bigger boat."

Roy Scheider, "Jaws",
film, directed by Steven Spielberg,
United States, produced by Richard D. Zanuck
& David Brown, 1975

"Frankly, my dear, I Don't give a damn."

Clark Gable, "Gone with the Wind",
film, directed by Victor Fleming,
United States, produced by David O. Selznick, 1939

"Lions, and tigers and bears, oh my! "

Judy Garland, "The Wizard of Oz",
film, directed by Victor Fleming, King Vidor,
United States, produced by Mervyn Leroy, 1939

"Toto, I've got a feeling
we're not in Kansas anymore."

Judy Garland, "The Wizard of Oz",
film, directed by Victor Fleming, King Vidor,
United States, produced by Mervyn Leroy, 1939

"There's no crying in baseball."

Tom Hanks, " A League of Their Own",
film, directed by Penny Marshall,
United States, produced by Robert Greenhut, 1992

"May the force be with you."

Alec Guinness, "Star Wars",
film, directed by George Lucas,
United States, produced by Lucasfilms, 1977

"The greatest trick the devil ever pulled
was convincing the world he didn't exist."

Kevin Spacey, "The Usual Suspects",
film, directed by Bryan Singer,
United States, produced by Polygram, 1992

"You've got to ask yourself one question:
Do I feel lucky? Well, punk, Do you, feel Lucky?"

Clint Eastwood, "Dirty Harry",
Film, directed by Don Siegel,
United States, produced by. Malpaso Productions, 1971

"You talkin' to me?"

Robert De Niro, "Taxi Driver",
film, directed by Martin Scorsese,
United States, produced by Julia Phillips, 1976

"This looks like the beginning
of a beautiful friendship."

Humphrey Bogart, "Casablanca"
film, directed by Michael Curtiz,
United States, produced by Hal B. Wallis, 1942

"Of all the gin joints in all the towns
in all the world, she walks into mine."

Humphrey Bogart,"Casablanca",
film, directed by Michael Curtiz,
United States, produced by Hal B. Wallis, 1942

"You can't handle the truth !"

Jack Nicholson, "A Few Good Men",
film, directed by Rob Reiner,
United States, produced by David Brown,
Andrew Scheinman, 1992

"The first rule of Fight Club is:
you don't talk about Fight Club."

*Brad Pitt, " Fight Club",
film, directed by David Fincher,
United States, produced by Art Linson,
Cean Chaffin, 1999*

"I am big! It's the pictures that got small."

*Gloria Swanson, "Sunset Boulevard",
film, directed by Billy Wilder,
United States, produced by Charles Brackett, 1950*

"I stopped thinking the way other people think
a long time ago. You gotta think like you think."

*Sylvester Stallone, "Rocky Balboa",
film, directed by Sylvester Stallone,
United States, produced by Irwin Winkler,
Robert Chartoff, 2006*

"Life is a banquet,
and most poor suckers are starving."

Rosalind Russell,
film, directed by Morton Dacosta,
United States, produced by Morton Dacosta, 1958

"Be on time, know your lines, and don,t bump into the furniture."

James Cagney on a note written to Michael J. Fox

CHAPTER TWENTY FIVE

Toasts and Speeches

"May you both live as long as you want and never want as long as you live."

"I've known many, liked a few,
loved only one - here's to you."

"Here's to my bride: she knows everything about me, yet she loves me just the same."

"There are good ships, and there are wood ships, and ships that sail the sea, but the best ships are friendships and may they always be."

Irish blessing

"Come grow old with me, the best is yet to be - the last of life for which the first was made."

Robert Browning

"May the wind be always at your back, may the sun shine warm upon your face, may the road rise up to meet you and may you be in heaven a half-hour before the devil knows your gone."

Irish Blessing

"It is better to have loved and lost than to have never loved at all."

Alfred Lord Tennyson

"Champagne for my real friends, real pain for my sham friends."

Francis Bacon

"To keep your marriage brimming with love...
whenever you're wrong: admit it.
Whenever you're right, shut up."

Ogden Nash

"Here's to nipples, for without them breasts would be pointless."

"I'll drink to the girl who will.
I'll drink to the girl who won't.
But I'll not drink to the girl who says she will,
but won't."

"There are old ships and new ships,
but the best ships are friendships.

"Here's to you and me."

"Immature love says 'I love you because I need you. Mature love says 'I need you because I love you.'"

Erich Fromm, philosopher

"If any of you are related to our main guests, let me know, so I can speak slowly."

Wendy Morgan, writer

"I don't want to be patronizing.... that means "talking down"."

Wendy Morgan, writer

"After such an introduction,
I can hardly wait to hear what
"I'm going to say."

Evelyn Andersen

"As my friend, Paul McCartney once said to me: 'Never be a name-dropper.'"

"A good speech like a woman's skirt, should be long enough to cover the subject and short enough to create interest."

"Once you get them laughing, they're listening and you can tell them almost anything."

Herb Gardner

"My father gave me these hints on speech making: Be sincere.... Be brief.... Be seated."

James Roosevelt

"Here's to those who wish us well, all the rest can go to hell."

"Be prompt, be short, be seated.

Franklin D. Roosevelt,
United States President, advice on speeches

"A graduation speaker is like a corpse
at an Irish wake.
You're supposed to show up and not say much."

U.S. Congressman "Tip" O'Neill

"I'm not afraid of tomorrow,
for I have seen yesterday and I love today."

William Allen White,
toasting himself on his 70th birthday.

"Here's to the nights we'll never remember, with the friends we'll never forget."

"Like the warmth of the sun and the light of the day,
may the luck of the Irish shine bright on your way."

Irish Toast

"May all your ups and downs be
between the sheets."

Wedding toast

THE END